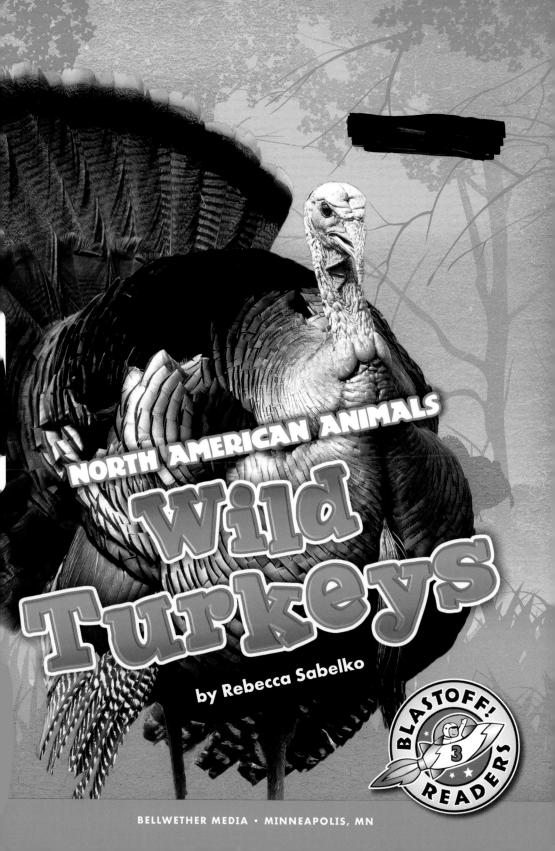

NORTH AMERICAN ANIMALS

Wild Turkeys

by Rebecca Sabelko

BLASTOFF!
3
READERS

BELLWETHER MEDIA • MINNEAPOLIS, MN

E5988

Note to Librarians, Teachers, and Parents:

Blastoff! Readers are carefully developed by literacy experts and combine standards-based content with developmentally appropriate text.

Level 1 provides the most support through repetition of high-frequency words, light text, predictable sentence patterns, and strong visual support.

Level 2 offers early readers a bit more challenge through varied simple sentences, increased text load, and less repetition of high-frequency words.

Level 3 advances early-fluent readers toward fluency through increased text and concept load, less reliance on visuals, longer sentences, and more literary language.

Level 4 builds reading stamina by providing more text per page, increased use of punctuation, greater variation in sentence patterns, and increasingly challenging vocabulary.

Level 5 encourages children to move from "learning to read" to "reading to learn" by providing even more text, varied writing styles, and less familiar topics.

Whichever book is right for your reader, Blastoff! Readers are the perfect books to build confidence and encourage a love of reading that will last a lifetime!

This edition first published in 2019 by Bellwether Media, Inc.

No part of this publication may be reproduced in whole or in part without written permission of the publisher. For information regarding permission, write to Bellwether Media, Inc., Attention: Permissions Department, 6012 Blue Circle Drive, Minnetonka, MN 55343.

Names: Sabelko, Rebecca, author.
Title: Wild Turkeys / by Rebecca Sabelko.
Description: Minnetonka, MN : Bellwether Media, Inc., 2019. | Series: Blastoff! Readers. North American Animals | Audience: Age 5-8. | Audience: K to Grade 3. | Includes bibliographical references and index.
Identifiers: LCCN 2018030416 (print) | LCCN 2018032390 (ebook) | ISBN 9781681036458 (ebook) | ISBN 9781626179141 (hardcover : alk. paper)
Subjects: LCSH: Wild turkey—Juvenile literature.
Classification: LCC QL696.G27 (ebook) | LCC QL696.G27 S23 2019 (print) | DDC 598.6/45–dc23
LC record available at https://lccn.loc.gov/2018030416

Editor: Kate Moening   Designer: Josh Brink
Printed in the United States of America, North Mankato, MN.

Table of Contents

What Are Wild Turkeys?

Wild turkeys are large, round birds. They live throughout the eastern and central United States and areas of the west.

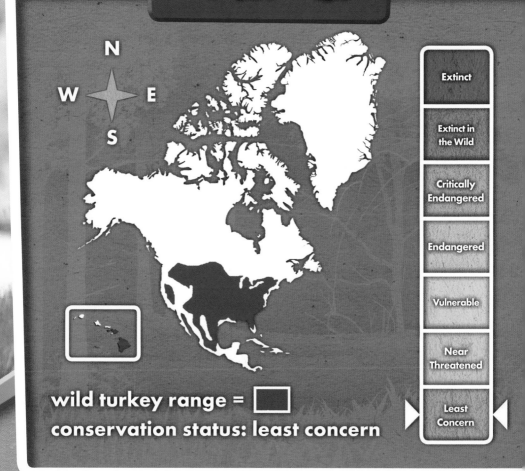

In the Wild

N
W — E
S

Extinct

Extinct in the Wild

Critically Endangered

Endangered

Vulnerable

Near Threatened

Least Concern

wild turkey range = ☐
conservation status: least concern

Some **flocks** are found as far north as southern Canada. Others live in parts of Mexico.

Wild turkeys look for food in forests filled with nut trees. They also gather in open fields.

These birds make their way into tree-filled yards, too. Sometimes, they are found along roads.

beard

Male wild turkeys have dark, shiny feathers. Their bald heads are blue.

8

long legs **bald head** **fanned tail**

Dark **beards** stick out from their chests. Their tails are a fan of feathers.

female

Females are smaller than males.
They are about 36 inches
(91 centimeters) long. Dark brown
feathers cover their bodies.
Their tails have a reddish shine.

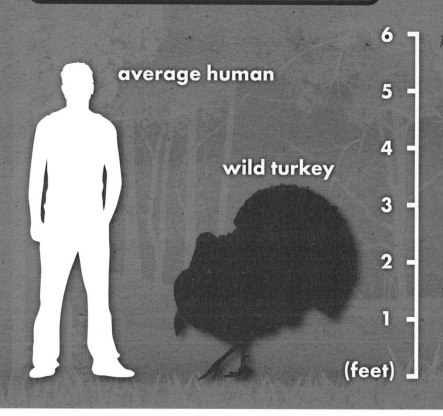

Size of a Wild Turkey

average human

wild turkey

6
5
4
3
2
1
(feet)

Both males and females have **snoods** that rest over their beaks. Red **wattles** hang from their necks.

Grinding Gizzards

Wild turkeys are **omnivores**. Their favorite foods are berries and nuts. They eat insects, too.

red oak acorns

hickory nuts

wild black
cherries

white ash seeds

American grasshoppers

earthworms

Their strong feet **scratch** away dead leaves as they search for food on the ground.

13

Wild turkeys swallow a lot of food.
It is stored in the **crop**. The crop
can store up to 1 pound
(0.4 kilograms) of food!

Food moves from the crop to the **gizzard**. Here, hard foods are broken into little pieces.

bobcats

golden eagles

great horned
owns

coyotes

mountain lions

raccoons

Many animals hunt wild turkeys.
But the turkeys' excellent
sight and hearing help them
spot **predators**.

16

Males often run from enemies.
Females tend to fly away.
They can fly up to 59 miles
(95 kilometers) per hour!

A Growing Flock

Each spring, females make
nests under brush or in tall grass.
There, they lay eggs. Females cluck
softly as the baby birds **hatch**.
The clucks help the **chicks** get
to know their mom.

Baby Facts

Name for babies:	chicks
Number of eggs laid:	4 to 17 eggs
Time spent inside egg:	25 to 31 days
Time spent with mom:	up to 10 months

Chicks quickly learn to peck for food. They listen for their mom's **alarm call** as they look for food.

By fall, the **poults** are ready to be part of the flock!

Glossary

alarm call—a sound an animal makes when in danger

beards—long feathers that grow on the chests of wild turkeys

chicks—baby wild turkeys

crop—a pouch inside the throats of many birds where food is stored

flocks—groups of wild turkeys

gizzard—a part of a bird's stomach where food is ground into small pieces

hatch—to break out of an egg

omnivores—animals that eat both plants and animals

poults—young wild turkeys

predators—animals that hunt other animals for food

scratch—to rub with something sharp or rough

snoods—flaps of skin that hang from the foreheads of wild turkeys

wattles—flaps of skin that hang from the necks of wild turkeys

To Learn More

AT THE LIBRARY
Graubart, Norman D. *How To Track A Turkey*.
New York, N.Y.: Windmill Books, 2015.

Magby, Meryl. *Wild Turkeys*. New York, N.Y.:
PowerKids Press, 2014.

Pendergast, George. *Turkey Hunting*. New York,
N.Y.: Gareth Stevens, 2015.

ON THE WEB

FACTSURFER

Factsurfer.com gives you
a safe, fun way to find
more information.

1. Go to www.factsurfer.com.

2. Enter "wild turkeys" into the search box.

3. Click the "Surf" button and select your
   book cover to see a list of related web sites.

Index